INTRODUCTION

This is my tenth and last book in the "Camera" series. On that account _____ ake it an all-colour book even though colour litho printing is more expensive th

It is now over fifty years since I began to photograph our city. It began _____, _____ ay after looking for something to point my new camera at. It soon became an engrossing hobby with many hours spent in the dark room developing negatives and making prints.

Not many of my early photographs were in colour, which was expensive both for film and subsequent processing, since few amateurs undertook the cost of processing colour. I certainly did not and since 35mm monochrome film could be bought in 50 and 100 foot reels and cut to length it was a relatively cheap form of photography.

Regrets that I have are many and usually are for opportunities missed. When I started out I could have photographed all the cinemas and theatres. I only managed to capture some of them but I have searched high and low for any photo of the Phoenix music hall - later cinema - on Langsett Road without success - not even a Brownie box photo seems to exist.

In concluding the series I would like to thank everyone at Pickards for their help and patience in getting the series under way. In particular I would like to thank Michael Liversidge of the company without whose help none of these little books would have been born. It was a chance meeting with him some seven years ago that led to his putting the idea of publishing some of my pictures into my head.

Lastly thanks to all who have bought my books and to those who have written with additional information or pointed out the occasional error.

You may hear from me again - God willing.

INDEX

The Sea Cadets' Band prepare to march off on Remembrance Sunday 1981. The location is Surrey Street.

Street trader Mr L, Knight selling apples on Dixon Lane in 1974.

Left: This little tobacconist's shop belonged to Mr Sutcliffe and was on Division Street. A photo in black and white is in my Sheffield Camera book. This is a different aspect.

This well-known corner of Fargate was to be ripped apart retaining only the frontage in the mid-1980s to create Orchard Square. The date here is 1974.

The Abbeydale Cinema on Abbeydale Road is here seen showing a James Bond film 'On Her Majesty's Secret Service'. The date is May 1970.

This dates back to 1968. There is Tudor Street in the foreground, Tudor Way to the right and Norfolk Street centre and left. The original Nether Chapel is the red building and the other large building was Wilk's hardware store with the Victoria Hall peeping above it. All of this is now Tudor Square.

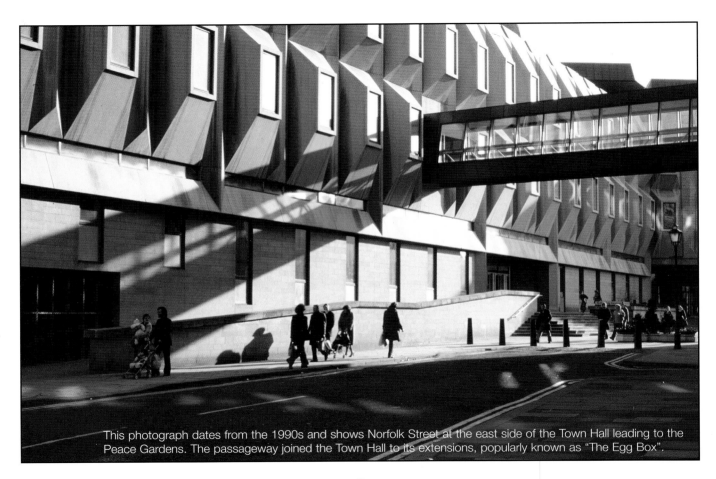

This photograph dates from the 1990s and shows Norfolk Street at the east side of the Town Hall leading to the Peace Gardens. The passageway joined the Town Hall to its extensions, popularly known as "The Egg Box".

This is a view of Parkwood Springs taken in 1968. The road in the foreground is Douglas Road. Every house here has now gone.

Sally's Tea shop was on Orchard Street near where it joins Leopold Street. The date is 1982 - a few years before this became part of Orchard Square.

Rumour has it that the Roebuck Tavern is to go. This fine old 18th century pub once stood on the fringes of the city but has gradually become submerged by new multi-storey neighbours. I hope it survives but like its neighbour the "Yorkshire Grey" it may be standing in the path of "progress".

Norwood Hall stood just off Herries Road. Norwood Avenue and Norwood Grange are the only memorials to this fine old building. It dated back to 1710 or thereabouts. In its later life it became the home of the Bishop of Sheffield, Dr Burrows. During the war it was used by the army. This photo dates from the 1970s by which time it had been neglected to such an extent that one night the council moved in and demolished it in spite of the fact that it was a listed building.

This was taken by climbing the steps at the side of the Royal Hospital on Westfield Terrace. Running to the left is Rockingham Street. The pub on the corner is the Foresters Inn. The temporary car park occupies land cleared of a number of small shop on Division Street. The date is 1975.

This thriving kiosk was to be found at the Exchange Street entrance to the Sheaf Market. It went some years ago to make way for the new flats that are being developed.

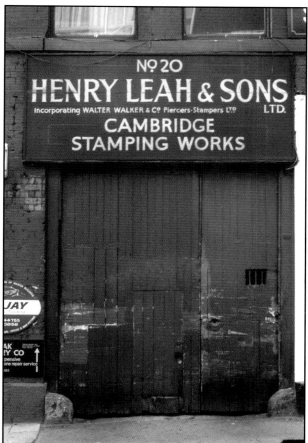

Left -
At No. 20 Cambridge Street this was the entrance to Leah's Yard - a lane of "little mester" workshops.

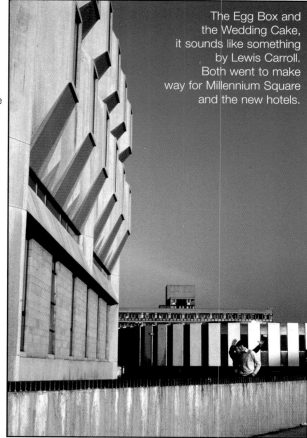

The Egg Box and the Wedding Cake, it sounds like something by Lewis Carroll. Both went to make way for Millennium Square and the new hotels.

This view of the Kelvin Flats was taken from Parkwood Springs.
The huge complex lasted for little more than thirty years before it was demolished.

The RSPCA animal sanctuary on Spring Street, familiarly known as the dogs' home, is here shown in its final days before demolition.

A tramcar passing the Manchester Hotel on Nursery Street. The pub was also known as the Manchester and Lincolnshire Railway Hotel due to its proximity to Bridgehouses Railway Station. The pub has now been renamed The Harlequin.

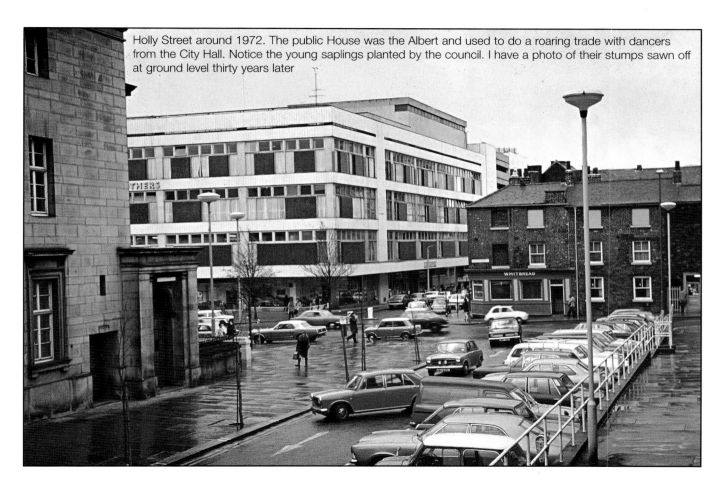

Holly Street around 1972. The public House was the Albert and used to do a roaring trade with dancers from the City Hall. Notice the young saplings planted by the council. I have a photo of their stumps sawn off at ground level thirty years later

Tudor Street has gone along with the two shops shown here, namely Jenkinson Marshall - stationers and H. Kirk - newsagent. This site is now part of Tudor Square. When I knew the stationers Bob Marshall was in charge assisted by his kindly lady assistants. Mr Marshall fought to save his shop but to no avail.

This is Bridgehouses when there were still houses to be seen. In the background can be seen part of the railway station. The date is 1968.

Luke Lane was part of the lost village of Wadsley. This dates from 1968. Later when plans to demolish most of the village were announced a "Save Our Village" campaign began without success. I thought at one time to include Wadsley in my "Camera" series but doubted that I had enough material, so here is a taster of what might have been.

Southey Hill is useful for capturing views of the area. On the left is the Ritz cinema after it became a Bingo Hall. At the moment its future seems uncertain. The road is Southey Green Road leading to Halifax Road - a road now notorious for its traffic calming bumps.

23

Bridge Street around 1980. Everything on the photograph has now gone with the exception of the facade of the brewery. The whole area on the left is covered with high rise flats.

Spring Street in the 1970s.
The building was the Britannia Works.
The blue door on the corner played a part in the
Sheffield Gang Wars. It was the home of
members of the Mooney family and was
attacked by a rival gang.

Flat Street to Fitzalan Square as it was in 1968. The pub was the Elephant Inn at the corner of Norfolk Street. Notice that the statue of Edward VII was on public view and not hidden by trees.

Bus strikes were a boon to taxi drivers. Back around 1980 taxis were allowed to park in the centre of Barker's Pool. Here stranded shoppers are in for a long wait for their tea.

Here is another one for the Parkwood Springs people. It shows Wallace Road running downhill towards the engine sheds with a terrace of back-to-backs.
The date is 1968.

Sheffield Sheaf Market familiarly known as the "rag and tag" looking towards the poultry market. The building with the arch was the original meat market but latterly became a place for market gardeners and others. The date is around 1968.

A view of Hillfoot School. The view is from Langsett Road looking towards Parkwood Springs in 1968.

A view of Sheaf Street, back in the 1950s. Interesting posters showing one that announces the closure of the Playhouse Theatre in Townhead Street. It is worth noting how many people arriving at the Midland station are carrying their luggage to the buses.

Left:
The Master Cutler stands at the Midland Station in the 1950s

Right:
This old music hall on West Bar went though many uses before it was demolished.

This high view of Rodgers' vast works is from above Sheaf Street showing where Pond Hill meets Sheaf Street with the bridge over the River Sheaf. The bus station was completely hidden behind the works when I took this photo in 1968.

The Botanical Gardens around 1980 before the grant from the Lottery led to a recent make-over.

The entrance on the left on Nursery Street led down steps to Quadraphenia - a retail hi-fi store. To the right is Blonk Street currently under massive reconstruction with high girders everywhere as I write this in December 2006.

A nostalgic view of Fargate around fifty years ago. The tramcar makes the picture - yes we used to call them that rather than the rather vulgar "trams".

Two from the 1950s.
On the left Barkers Pool and on the right the pleasant walk through the old Peace Gardens opposite Pinstone Street.

The bus station as it was in the late 1950s with a view of Park Hill.

Another view of Douglas Road showing the lower part where it bends to go under the railway viaduct. Same date as previously - 1968.

Crookes Valley boating lake back in 1957.

This is how Division Street was in 1975. The Fire Station was on the right before the new one on Charter Square replaced it.

The Netherthorpe roundabout is now nearing its fiftieth birthday. Here is how it all started with this tiny circus. Since then its diameter has grown massively and even a tunnel for supertram has been created beneath it.

Another corner of the Peace Gardens taken over twenty years ago in a more peaceful age - no fountains, just grass and trees in this winter scene.

This is Barker's Pool and the war memorial before its renovation. The bus on the left has special dispensation to encroach on this pedestrian area in order to persuade you to donate your organs for transplants. The trees seen here are on death row along with all the others that were on Holly Street and Balm Green. No doubt you will have your opinions on whether the new layout is an improvement - I certainly have.

The Nag's Head pub on Shalesmoor is no more. It was demolished fairly recently to make way for the new ring road.

A night shot of Arundel Gate taken in 1983. The Sheffield Registry office in the shape of a wedding cake is on the right.

This view of Castlegate and Blonk Street, although dating from only a few years ago is undergoing vast alterations even as I write this. On both sides of Blonk Street huge girder constructions have arisen and the buildings to be seen on the banks of the River Don seem destined for demolition.

Fargate now has a Continental Market from time to time. One determined lady knows exactly what she wants.

The Pierrotters claim to be the last Pierrot troupe still in existence. Such groups were quite common on the sands at seaside resorts before the First World War. I was part of the audience in the Winter Gardens when they performed at the opening of Millennium Square.

The Iraq War is one of the major disasters of this new millennium. This protest march in Leopold Street took place shortly after the war began.

The entrance to Ponds Forge on Sheaf Street before it was engulfed by the swimming baths. There have been other shots of this but none, I think, in colour. Notice the contradictory road-signs - "entrance only" and "turn left on exit".

Even as I write (Christmas 2006) a huge alteration has taken place to the Midland Station entrance and the area to its front.
This is how it looked in 1968.

This view of Bridgehouses in the 1960s is now almost completely transformed. On the left was the station approach. On the right a car is seen entering Corporation Street and centre left is the River Don where it passes Nursery Street.

When the Wednesday reached the play-offs for promotion, to The Championship, I caught this street vendor with his Wednesday favours promoting the "March on Cardiff" - the venue for the play-off. In case there is a Rip-Van-Winkle out there I should say that the march was a success

Arundel Gate in the 1990s before the "eggbox" and the "wedding cake" were demolished to make for Winter Gardens and the new hotel.

The corner of Haymarket and High Street in the early 1970s. John Collier was a tailor chain that did much advertising on television with their slogan "John Collier, John Collier - the window to watch".

An early morning shot of London Road in 1968. In the distance is Lowfields School and on the right at Nelson's pianos is Fieldhead Rd.

The bottom of the Moor was being effectively blocked off in 1980 by the building of the Manpower Services offices.

Rutland Road viewed from the footbridge that once crossed Pitsmoor Road to the flats. Both flats and footbridge have now gone as has the school. The date is 1968 - a date that recurs throughout the book when I was taking colour slides by courtesy of Gratispool - who provided a service whereby the slides were returned together with a new film.
Unfortunately some of them are beginning to deteriorate so that I am having to convert them to digital images asap.

The new City Hall rises like a Phoenix from the ashes following its restoration. I have yet to see the inside of the building not being a pop fan.

A view between Penistone Road and Infirmary Road with the Kelvin Flats in the distance. The date is 1980.

A requiem here for all the corner shops of my childhood. Every district had one where we could go to spend our ha'pennies but one by one they were demolished or were converted into houses. This survivor is at the corner of Ben Lane and Studfield Hill.

A view of Pond Street in the 1950s when development was beginning to take place.

This photograph shows the point where Infirmary Road becomes Shalesmoor. The pub centre left is at the junction of Penistone Road and Cornish Street (see next page). To the right was the Roscoe cinema (not visible). The old house on the left was once the surgery of Dr. Charles B. Anderson and occupied a prominent position at the junction of four roads. Nothing now remains of this scene.

This shows Cornish Street at its junction with Shalesmoor in the 1960s. James Dixon's works can be seen in the distance.

This view of Shude Hill looking towards Pond Street was taken from Commercial Street which was possible back in 1968.

Fletchers' name was synonymous with bread in my younger days and their vans toured the city. By the time this photo was taken the firm had become Fletcher's Fresh and Frozen Foods before a recent disastrous fire gutted the entire building. The site is on Claywheels Lane, Wadsley Bridge.

Castle Square before we lost the "hole-in-the-road" to Supertram. The two stores have both gone - C & A Modes and Waring and Gillow. The date was 1980s.

The Wicker as viewed from the Wicker Arches. The photo was taken in 1974 following the dismantling of the Wicker Station when I was carrying out a bit of Industrial archaeology.

This block of shops was between Surrey Street and Norfolk Row - a site that has recently been redeveloped. Music lovers will remember Bradley's Records in the days of the long-playing record. The date is 1980.

A Peace Gardens panorama taken fairly recently but before the new and controversial hotel was built. It was a particularly warm summer day and the new features were proving popular. Not many people now remember the old St. Paul's church. The late Joe and Betty Weston certainly did for they were married there. Joe won the plunge championship so regularly that they eventually gave him the cup and his wife Betty often sang from Sheffield in the early days of broadcasting. Sheffield swimmers will remember them well.

The entrance to Newton Chambers shown here was approached from the Warren end. The firm dominated Chapeltown. They owned many of the local houses and were the main employer in the town. We never dreamed they would disappear so quickly. Modern houses now occupy the site.

This terrace of houses was on Douglas Road. I find it full of interest. It was taken in 1968 so the lady standing in her doorway is probably of a good age or has passed away. Who was she? I love her pinafore (pinnie was the usual name) - it reminds me of my youth in the 1930s. Notice the cellar grates. All the older houses had coal cellars. There was nothing more cheerful than a coal fire with its red, yellow and blue patterns - more watchable and heart-warming than much of today's television.

This Pitsmoor view of the car wash on Chatham Street with its view of the flats will be remembered by many. Demolition has taken place for the new ring road currently under construction.

This view from Granville Street shows Pond Street in the early stages of its re-development back in the 1950s looking over the Midland Station.

The white building here was Chapeltown House. It was demolished in the late 1960s but the attached cottage was stoutly defended by the Late Mr Marshall until he died when it was added to the new bank that had replaced the house. Everything here has now disappeared. This is a 1967 photo.

These shops at the corner of Longley Lane and Herries Road were fronted onto cottages known as Piper Cottages. Herries Road was Piper Lane before widening took place - hence the name of the cottages.

These ladies were busy in the Peace Gardens sewing for "Peace".

The photograph tells all except the date which was 1984.

This view of the Georgian terrace on Surrey Street was made possible following the demolition of buildings for the Eggbox site. On the left is the art shop, then the City Analyst's and Clarke's - the cleaners. Buildings on the extreme right were demolished and those that weren't now house Starbuck's coffee house. The date is around 1970